KILLER SPIDERS

Alex Woolf

W

FRANKLIN WATTS
LONDON • SYDNEY

This paperback edition published in 2014 by Franklin Watts

Franklin Watts
338 Euston Road
London NW1 3BH

Franklin Watts Australia
Level 17/207 Kent Street, Sydney, NSW 2000

Produced by Arcturus Publishing Limited,
26/27 Bickels Yard, 151–153 Bermondsey Street, London SE1 3HA

Series concept: Alex Woolf
Editor and picture researcher: Alex Woolf
Designer: Ian Winton

Picture credits
Nature Picture Library: 6 (Ingo Arndt), 11 (Alex Hyde), 12 (Adrian Davies), 13 (Stephen Dalton), 15 (Hans Christoph Kappel), 17 *bottom* (Wegner/ARCO), 21 (Stephen Dalton), 22 (Premaphotos), 23 (Premaphotos), 26 (Ingo Arndt), 27 (Ingo Arndt).
Shutterstock: 4 (Sebastian Duda), 5 (vblinov), 7 *top* (kotomiti), 9 (Damian Herde), 10 (Dirk Ercken), 16 (FikMik), 17 *top* (zshunfa), 18 (James van den Broek), 20 (Dr Morley Read), 25 (Cathy Keifer), 28 *top* (Sue Robinson), 28 *bottom* (Henrik Larsson), 29 (orionmystery@flickr).
Wikimedia Commons: 7 *bottom* (WillWig), 8 (Chuck Evans), 14 (Davefoc), 19 (shannon mccoll), 24 (Kaldari).

Every attempt has been made to clear copyright. Should there be any inadvertent omission, please apply to the publisher for rectification.

A CIP catalogue record for this book is available from the British Library.

Dewey Decimal Classification Number: 595.4'41566

ISBN 978 1 4451 3111 5

Printed in China

Franklin Watts is a division of Hachette Children's Books, an Hachette UK company.
www.hachette.co.uk

SL001711UK
Supplier 03, Date 0114, Print Run 3219

Contents

Death on Eight Legs

Spiders are scary-looking beasts, and many people are terrified of them. In fact, humans have little to fear from most spiders. But in the bug world, spiders are fearsome and deadly predators.

Tarantulas are large, hairy spiders that live in warm climates. They look monstrous and some are the size of dinner plates, but they rarely bite humans.

SNACK ON THIS!

There are about 40,000 spider species that we know about, and probably thousands more that we haven't discovered yet.

Spiders are not insects. They belong to a group of creatures called arachnids, which also includes scorpions, mites and ticks.

Most spiders kill or paralyse their prey by injecting venom. They then pump the victim's body with digestive juices that turn its insides to liquid. The spider sucks up the liquid, leaving an empty husk behind.

Spider facts

- **Life span:** 1-2 years on average, but tarantulas can live up to 25 years in captivity.

- **Lives in:** Every continent except Antarctica, and in most habitats, including mountains, rainforests, deserts and underground caves.

- **Eats:** Mainly insects and other spiders, but some larger spiders eat small birds, lizards and fish.

Spiders and their Webs

Spiders have special organs in their bodies called spinnerets that produce threads of silk. Spiders use silk as a safety line to move from place to place, and as a cocoon for their eggs. Many spiders also use the silk threads to build webs, so they can catch their prey.

Webs come in many shapes and sizes. These include orb webs, tangle webs, tubular webs, sheet webs and tent webs.

SNACK ON THIS!

Spider silk is just 1/200th of a millimetre wide. It's so light that if a spider spun a strand around the world, it would weigh just 170 grams.

An orb weaver spider spins a thread of silk. The spinnerets are at the rear of its abdomen.

When an insect flies into a web, the spider feels the vibration in the threads and it knows that it has caught its next meal!

The most famous type of spider's web is the orb web. It is made up of non-sticky straight threads running from the centre to the edge, and sticky spiral threads, for catching prey.

CHEW ON THAT!

In 1973, two orb weaver spiders were taken aboard the space station Skylab, to see if they could spin webs in zero gravity. After a few days, they adapted to the conditions. Space webs turned out to be finer than Earth webs.

The silver argiope spider, from the Americas, is famous for the dense zigzags it incorporates within its web.

Black Widows and Redbacks

Widow spiders are found in many of the warmer regions of the world. Two of the most famous kinds are the black widow spider, which lives in the desert regions of the south-western United States, and the redback, which lives in Australia.

The female black widow guards her egg case. Each case contains up to 750 eggs.

SNACK ON THIS!

Female black widows will sometimes kill and eat the male after they mate. Redback females have even been known to start eating the male while they are still mating!

The black widow is the most venomous spider in North America. Its venom is 15 times more toxic than that of a rattlesnake. Yet it rarely kills humans because it injects only a tiny amount of poison when it bites. Only the female black widow is dangerous to humans.

The black widow spins cobwebs — messy tangles of sticky silken threads. Its silk is among the strongest of all spider silks. It builds its webs on the underside of ledges, rocks and plants. Then it hangs upside down and waits for an insect to wander in.

Black widow facts

- **Length:** 2.5-3.8 cm
- **Lifespan:** 18 months
- **Eats:** Insects such as ants, cockroaches and beetles

The redback is regarded as one of the most dangerous spiders in Australia. As well as insects, it has been known to eat larger animals such as trapdoor spiders and lizards.

Net-Casting Spiders

Net-casting spiders have a unique method of catching their prey. Instead of waiting for insects to fly into their webs, they throw their webs over the insects!

When hunting, the spider hangs, head downwards, holding its web in its four front legs. When it sees an insect passing beneath, it lunges downwards and traps the insect in its web. The spider then wraps extra silk around its victim before injecting it with venom.

When its prey approaches, the spider stretches the web to two or three times its relaxed size, and gets ready to pounce.

SNACK ON THIS!

Net-casters are often called ogre-faced spiders, because they are said to look a lot like ogres!

The net-caster has very good vision. It has eight eyes, arranged in three rows. Two of its eyes are extremely large and are well-adapted for seeing at night.

The net-casting spider hunts at night. During the day it builds its web, which is rectangular and about the size of a postage stamp. The web is made of non-sticky, woolly silk. Insects get entangled in the fluffy threads.

Net-casting spider facts

- **Length:** 1.5-2.5 cm
- **Lives in:** Tropical lands, including Australia, Africa and the Americas
- **Eats:** Beetles, ants, crickets, spiders and moths

Water Spiders

The water spider is brown in colour, but the air bubble it carries on its furry abdomen while swimming gives it a silvery appearance.

The water spider, also known as the diving bell spider, lives almost its entire life underwater. It breathes by trapping air in a bubble held by the small hairs on its abdomen and legs.

The spider builds air-filled underwater webs. These are like diving bells – dome-shaped and open at the bottom. They are anchored to nearby plants by silken threads.

SNACK ON THIS!

When it wants to mate, the male water spider constructs a diving bell next to a female's, then builds a tunnel to hers, breaking through the wall of her web to gain access.

12

The water spider with its diving-bell web. The web is built in such a way that it can receive oxygen from the surrounding water, and expel carbon dioxide, so that the air inside remains breathable for long periods.

The spider makes its diving bell by spinning a sheet of silk underwater. It then collects air from the surface on its furry abdomen, and transports this to its underwater home. When the web is complete, the spider moves in.

The water spider sits in its diving bell waiting for its prey. When an insect touches the web or one of its anchoring strands, the spider darts out and catches it.

Water spider facts

- **Length:** 8-15 mm
- **Lives in:** Lakes, ponds and streams in temperate parts of Europe and Asia
- **Eats:** Aquatic insects, including midge larvae, water mites and mayfly nymphs

Trapdoor Spiders

The trapdoor spider does not build a web. Instead it uses its powerful jaws to dig a tube-shaped burrow in the earth, which it lines with silk.

Trapdoor spider facts

- **Lives in:** South-East Asia, China and Japan
- **Size:** Up to 4 cm long
- **Life span:** 1-2 years

It takes a trapdoor spider 6 to 12 hours to dig its burrow.

It closes the burrow entrance with a trapdoor, using silk as a hinge, and plant and soil materials to camouflage it.

The trapdoor spider puts its front pair of legs against the trapdoor and waits. The hairs on its body are very sensitive to vibration. When an insect wanders by, it feels the vibration, and shoots out of its burrow to catch it.

Some types of trapdoor spider lay silken 'trip lines' around their burrow. When an insect disturbs one of these lines, the spider is alerted, and rushes out.

A trapdoor spider emerges from its burrow. Despite its eight eyes, it has poor eyesight, and relies on its sensitivity to vibration to catch its prey.

SNACK ON THIS!

Trapdoor spiders are preyed on by spider wasps. When the wasp finds a burrow, she paralyses the spider with her sting, then lays an egg on the body. When the egg hatches, the larva eats the spider alive.

Tarantulas

Tarantulas are found in tropical and desert regions of the world, including South America, southern Europe, Africa, southern Asia and Australia.

The tarantula is feared by many people because of its large, hairy legs and body. This spider is, however, virtually harmless to humans. Its bite may be painful, but its venom is milder than a bee's.

SNACK ON THIS!

When threatened by another animal, tarantulas kick off a cloud of tiny, hooked hairs from their abdomen. The hairs land on the animal's skin, making it feel itchy and sore.

Most tarantulas live in burrows, but some live in trees in a silken tube-shaped 'tent'. They hunt at night, feeding mainly on insects, though larger tarantulas target bigger prey, including frogs, lizards, mice and even small snakes. The bird-eating spider, as its name suggests, sometimes feeds on young birds, which it steals from nests.

CHEW ON THAT!

The biggest tarantula - and also the world's biggest spider - is the goliath spider, which can be up to 12 centimetres long, and 28 centimetres across. It lives in the coastal rainforests of South America.

A tarantula (above) in its burrow, awaiting its next meal.

A tarantula eats a grasshopper. The spider's venomous bite paralyses its victim. Then it pours digestive juices into the grasshopper's body. This turns the insect's inner organs into a liquid soup, which the tarantula then sucks up.

Funnel-Web Spiders

Funnel-webs are highly venomous spiders found in south-eastern Australia. The most infamous of these is the Sydney funnel-web, which can be very aggressive and has caused a number of human deaths.

The Sydney funnel-web spider is regarded as one of the most dangerous spiders in the world. It will attack if it feels threatened. Unusually for spiders, the male is more dangerous than the female.

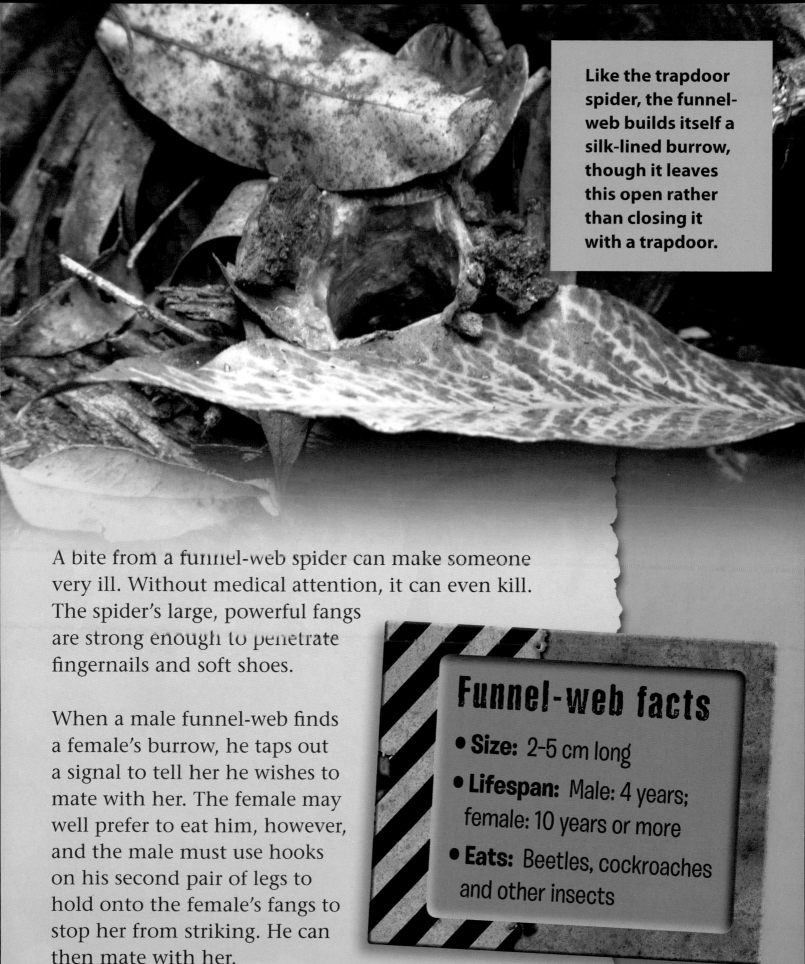

Like the trapdoor spider, the funnel-web builds itself a silk-lined burrow, though it leaves this open rather than closing it with a trapdoor.

A bite from a funnel-web spider can make someone very ill. Without medical attention, it can even kill. The spider's large, powerful fangs are strong enough to penetrate fingernails and soft shoes.

When a male funnel-web finds a female's burrow, he taps out a signal to tell her he wishes to mate with her. The female may well prefer to eat him, however, and the male must use hooks on his second pair of legs to hold onto the female's fangs to stop her from striking. He can then mate with her.

Funnel-web facts

- **Size:** 2-5 cm long
- **Lifespan:** Male: 4 years; female: 10 years or more
- **Eats:** Beetles, cockroaches and other insects

Spiders that Chase

A wolf spider feeds on a centipede. The spider's excellent eyesight and high sensitivity to vibrations make it an effective hunter.

Some spiders don't sit and wait for their prey to come to them, but actively hunt. These include the wolf spider and the spitting spider.

The wolf spider lives in burrows and hunts at night. It will lurk in a concealed spot and wait for its victim to come near, then chase it down. Some wolf spiders even jump in the air to catch flying insects.

SNACK ON THIS!

On a good night a wolf spider can catch and eat up to 15 insects.

Unlike other spider species, the mother wolf spider carries her egg sac around with her, attached to the end of her abdomen. Despite this, she is able to continue hunting.

The spitting spider has a unique way of hunting. The spider's venom glands also produce a sticky kind of silk, which it spits at its victims.

As it spits it sways from side to side so that the spit comes out in two zigzags – one from each fang. These strings of spit glue the victim to the spot. The spider then moves in and gives its immobilized prey a venomous bite.

A spitting spider is about to fire its sticky spit at a mosquito.

CHEW ON THAT!

A spitting spider attack lasts just a little under 1/700th of a second.

Wandering Spiders

Unlike the wolf spider, which waits for its victims to come close before chasing them down, the wandering spider moves about in search of prey. It is a night hunter, and is extremely sensitive to sounds, smells and vibrations.

One of the largest wandering spiders is the rusty, found in the rainforests of Costa Rica, where it preys on tree frogs and lizards. It can be up to 15 centimetres across.

A rusty wandering spider tucks into a tree frog.

Wandering spider facts

- **Lives in:** The forests of South America
- **Size:** 13-15 cm across
- **Eats:** Crickets and other large insects, small lizards, frogs and mice

Wandering spiders are so-called because they do not live in a burrow or web, but wander the forest floor. They can move very quickly, and are highly aggressive. Unlike most spider species, they do not run away when challenged, but stand their ground.

SNACK ON THIS!

Wandering spiders can hear through sense organs on their legs.

A female Brazilian wandering spider guards her egg sac, which she has camouflaged with bits of dead leaf.

Especially dangerous is the Brazilian wandering spider, one of the most deadly spiders in the world. This spider sometimes enters houses and hides in shoes or other items of clothing. Its bite is extremely painful, and its venom is powerful enough to kill a human, if not treated quickly.

Jumping Spiders

As its name suggests, the jumping spider is an aerial hunter, leaping on its victims before killing and eating them. A daytime hunter, it actively stalks its prey, rather than relying on a web or ambush.

Jumping spiders have excellent vision, not only for hunting but also for courtship. The males tend to be colourful to attract the attention of females.

SNACK ON THIS!

Jumping spiders can climb the smoothest surfaces, including glass. They can do this because the tips of their legs subdivide into thousands of tiny hairs, each tipped with an 'end foot'.

When the jumping spider has located its victim, it positions itself within jumping range, and then creates a dragline. This is a strand of silk that it tethers to another object, so that if the spider misses its prey, it doesn't fall.

A jumping spider eats a fruit fly.

The jumping spider can leap up to 20 times its own length. It does this by using its abdominal muscles, which force liquid into its rear legs, hurling the spider forwards.

Jumping spiders can be crafty. The fringed jumping spider of Australia and South-East Asia preys on web-building spiders. It uses its legs to vibrate the web, fooling the spider into thinking it has caught prey. When it rushes out, the fringed jumping spider leaps on it.

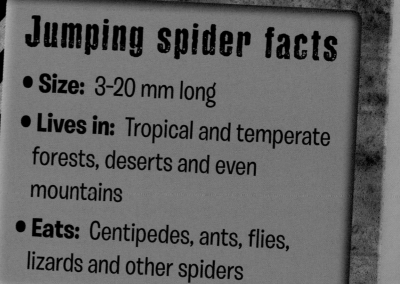

Jumping spider facts

- **Size:** 3-20 mm long
- **Lives in:** Tropical and temperate forests, deserts and even mountains
- **Eats:** Centipedes, ants, flies, lizards and other spiders

Fishing Spiders

The fishing spider is found near ponds and slow-moving streams. It hunts by using the water surface like a web, with the ripples of the water telling it an insect has landed nearby.

The spider holds onto the shore with its rear legs and extends the rest of its body on the water surface. The hairs on the spider's legs and feet are amazingly sensitive and can tell the difference, for example, between the splash of a twig falling on the water and the vibration made by a struggling insect.

Fishing spider facts

- **Size:** Up to 12 cm across
- **Lives in:** Americas, Europe and New Zealand
- **Eats:** Mayflies and other aquatic insects, as well as small fish

The fishing spider is able to float on water because of the fine, air-trapping hairs all over its body.

When prey is detected, the fishing spider races towards it, across the water surface. It overpowers its victims with its claw-tipped forelegs, before biting them.

The fishing spider can also climb beneath the surface of the water. Its velvety, unwettable hairs trap a bubble of air around its body, much like the water spider. It breathes this air as it fishes. The air makes it very buoyant, so it must anchor itself to a plant stem if it wishes to remain underwater.

A fishing spider from French Guiana goes to work on a fish.

SNACK ON THIS!

When a fishing spider surfaces after an underwater hunting expedition, the air bubble around its body bursts and the spider emerges completely dry.

Camouflage and Mimicry

Some spiders hunt by using camouflage – using their colouring to blend into the background. Others get their food by mimicry – pretending to be another creature altogether.

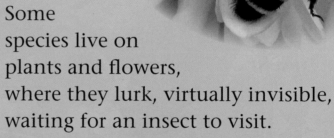

The crab spider is very small – often less than a centimetre long – and is a master of camouflage. Some species live on plants and flowers, where they lurk, virtually invisible, waiting for an insect to visit.

Another type, the bark crab spider, is coloured – you guessed it! – like bark. One type of crab spider even looks like bird droppings!

This flower crab spider (right) is so well camouflaged, you can barely see it – and neither did the bee!

This wolf spider (below) is very well camouflaged against a tree.

SNACK ON THIS!

Some types of crab spider can even change colour to match their background.

Some jumping spiders mimic ants. They have long, slender legs and what appears to be a three-part insect body. To add to the disguise, they often raise their forelegs in the air like a pair of antennae.

The spiders may do this to prey on the ants they are mimicking, or else on the tiny bugs that live with the ants. Another theory is that the spiders mimic ants to avoid being eaten by predators such as spider-hunting wasps.

CHEW ON THAT!

In the case of one African species of jumping spider, the baby spiders imitate one speces of ant, while the mature spiders imitate another completely different ant species.

An ant-mimicking jumping spider preys on a winged ant.

Glossary

abdomen The rear section of a spider, where its heart, liver, lungs and silk-producing organs are located.

aerial Operating in, or coming out of, the air.

ambush Launch a surprise attack from a concealed position.

antennae A pair of long, thin sensory appendages on the heads of insects.

aquatic Dwelling in or near water.

buoyant Able to float.

camouflage An animal's natural colouring or form that enables it to blend in with its surroundings.

carbon dioxide A gas that animals produce when they breathe out.

cocoon A silky case spun by spiders to protect their young.

courtship The process by which male animals try to attract a mate.

diving bell An open-bottomed chamber that, when lowered underwater, keeps the air trapped inside the bell.

dragline A thread of silk produced by a jumping spider to act as a safety line when leaping through the air.

egg sac A protective silk pouch in which a female spider puts her eggs.

gland An organ in human or animal bodies that produces chemical substances for a particular purpose.

habitat A creature's natural environment.

immobilized Prevented from moving.

larva The young form of an insect.

mimicry The action of imitating something.

organ A part of the body that performs a particular function.

oxygen A gas that forms part of the air. Animals must breathe oxygen to live.

paralyse Cause a person or animal to become partly or wholly incapable of movement.

predator An animal that preys on other animals.

prey An animal that is hunted and killed by another animal for food.

primate A type of mammal that includes monkeys, apes and humans.

species A group of living organisms that are similar enough to interbreed.

spiral Winding in a continuous and gradually widening curve around a central point.

toxic Poisonous; harmful.

trip lines Silk threads positioned outside a spider's burrow so that insects will brush against them, alerting the spider to their presence.

tropical Of the tropics – the warmest region of the Earth, close to the equator.

tubular Long, round and hollow, like a tube.

venom Poisonous fluid injected by some predators into their prey.

Further Information

Books

Amazing Animals: Spiders by Sally Morgan (Franklin Watts, 2011)

Killer Nature: Scary Spiders by Lynn Huggins-Cooper (Franklin Watts, 2008)

Spiders of the World by Rod and Ken Preston-Mafham (Facts on File, 2003)

Usborne Beginners: Spiders by Rebecca Gilpin (Usborne, 2007)

Wild Predators: Deadly Spiders and Scorpions by Andrew Solway (Heinemann, 2005)

Websites

animals.howstuffworks.com/arachnids/spider6.htm
All about spider anatomy and behaviour.

www.biokids.umich.edu/critters/Arachnida/
Information about spiders and their relatives, plus pictures.

news.nationalgeographic.com/news/2004/06/0623_040623_ spiderfacts.html
Fascinating spider facts.

www.the-piedpiper.co.uk/th11f.htm
Simple information about spiders, including pages on individual species.

www.wisegeek.com/what-are-the-worlds-deadliest-spiders.htm
Information about highly venomous spiders.

Index

Page numbers in **bold** refer to pictures.